WILLIAM MORRIS

PEPIN®

GIFT & CREATIVE PAPERS

VOLUME

67

English

William Morris

William Morris (1834–1896) famously quoted that every individual should 'Have nothing in your house that you do not know to be useful, or believe to be beautiful', that he based his working career on that quote says much for the man as an individual, and much for the legacy of his creative output.

William Morris was one of the most important and influential of English decorative designers of the nineteenth century. His design work was prodigious, producing hundreds of designs for printed and woven textiles, embroidery, tapestry, wallpaper, stained glass, book decoration and more. His pattern work has endured in popularity and has been a favourite with the general public, interior designers, and craftspeople across the generations.

As is evident in his work, Morris had an abiding affinity with the natural world. In many respects, his pattern work was a celebration of the endless variety that can be found in the English countryside. Although by no means the only designer who took nature as his personal creative template, Morris was certainly one of the most successful. It was his intrinsic understanding of the beauty to be found in nature, and how that beauty could be processed and then naturally stylised within a decorative pattern, that made Morris one of the most successful of Victorian designers.

It is the obvious intimacy, recognition, and admiration that Morris had for the natural world that comes across so vividly in his decorative work, from his initial designs of the 1860s, right through till the end of his life in the 1890s. The colours, the lines, the styles of his work emphasised a direct connection with nature, and it is this that made his work such a draw for so many in the nineteenth century. As cities expanded and the natural world retreated, Morris vibrant and engaging pattern work was the only real connection many had with nature. It is no wonder that so many Victorians covered their homes with Morris decorative pattern work, in some ways it brought the colour, movement, and vibrancy of nature into the home.

This is why so much of Morris decorative work has stayed with us, and why it is still as popular as it ever was. We can see the love Morris had for nature, the real connections that he was able to make. His admiration of nature endures, and through that we are able to join with him in that admiration.

Français

William Morris

William Morris (1834–1896) aurait déclaré : « N'ayez rien dans votre maison qui ne soit, à votre connaissance, utile, ou que vous n'estimiez comme beau ». Le fait que sa carrière professionnelle se soit fondée sur cette citation en dit long sur l'homme en tant que tel, et encore plus sur la production créative qu'il nous a laissée en héritage.

William Morris était l'un des designers décoratifs anglais les plus importants et les plus influents du XIXe siècle. Son travail en matière de design fut prodigieux : il a produit des centaines de modèles pour les textiles imprimés et tissés, la broderie, la tapisserie, le papier peint, les vitraux, la décoration de livres et bien d'autres choses encore. Son travail sur les motifs est encore extrêmement populaire et il suscite un vif intérêt auprès du grand public, des architectes d'intérieur et des artisans à travers les générations.

Tel qu'en fait foi son travail, Morris avait une grande affinité avec le monde de la nature. À bien des égards, son travail sur les motifs était une célébration de l'infinie variété qu'on peut trouver dans la campagne anglaise. Bien qu'il ne soit pas, de loin, le seul designer à avoir pris la nature comme modèle pour ses créations personnelles, Morris fut certainement l'un des plus brillants. C'est sa compréhension intrinsèque de la beauté inhérente à la nature, et la façon dont cette beauté pouvait être traitée, puis stylisée naturellement en un motif décoratif, qui a fait de Morris l'un des designers victoriens à avoir connu le plus grand succès.

C'est de toute évidence la familiarité, la reconnaissance et l'admiration de Morris pour le monde naturel qu'il exprime de façon si frappante à travers son travail de décoration, ses premiers dessins des années 1860, et ce, jusqu'à la fin de sa vie, dans les années 1890. Les couleurs, les lignes, les styles de son travail soulignaient un lien direct avec la nature, d'où l'incroyable succès remporté par son travail au XIXe siècle. Avec la croissance des villes et le recul du monde sauvage, le caractère vivant et attachant des motifs de Morris était pour beaucoup leur seul lien réel avec la nature. Il n'est donc pas étonnant qu'à l'époque victorienne, tant de gens aient recouvert les murs de leurs maisons de motifs décoratifs de Morris. D'une certaine façon, ils apportaient à leurs foyers la couleur, le mouvement et la vie de la nature.

C'est pour cette raison que tant d'œuvres décoratives de Morris sont encore des nôtres, et que sa popularité n'a jamais décliné. Son travail témoigne de l'amour qu'éprouvait Morris pour la nature et pour les véritables liens qu'il était capable d'établir avec elle. Son admiration pour la nature perdure et, à travers celle-ci, nous sommes en mesure de nous joindre à lui dans cette admiration.

William Morris.

Textile printing and weaving at the William Morris & Co.

Deutsch

William Morris

Ein berühmtes Zitat von William Morris (1834–1896) besagt, dass niemand, etwas in seinem Haus haben sollte, das ihm nicht nützlich ist oder er nicht für schön hält'. Danach arbeitete er – was viel über den Mann als Person und über seine kreative Hinterlassenschaft aussagt.
William Morris war einer der wichtigsten und einflussreichsten englischen Gestalter und Kunsthandwerker des 19. Jahrhunderts. Zu seinen wundervollen Arbeiten gehörten hunderte verschiedener Entwürfe für bedruckte, gewebte und bestickte Stoffe, Wandbehänge, Tapeten, Glasmalereien, Buchschmuck und anderes. Seine Muster sind immer populär und über viele Generationen beim breiten Publikum, bei Innenausstattern und Kunsthandwerkern beliebt geblieben.
In seinen Arbeiten wird offensichtlich, dass Morris eine beständige Affinität zur Natur hatte. Die von ihm entworfenen Muster zelebrierten in vieler Hinsicht die endlose Vielfalt, die Englands Natur und Landschaft zu bieten hatten. Morris war bei weitem nicht der einzige Gestalter, der sich die Natur zur persönlichen Vorlage machte, aber sicherlich einer der erfolgreichsten. Er hatte in seinem tiefsten Innern verstanden, welche Schönheit die Natur in sich barg und wie sich diese Schönheit umsetzen und natürlich zu einem dekorativen Muster stilisieren ließ. Das machte ihn zu einem der erfolgreichsten Designer des Viktorianischen Zeitalters.
Die offensichtliche Vertrautheit, Anerkennung und Bewunderung, die Morris für die Natur empfand, wird bereits in der Ornamentik seiner ersten Entwürfen aus den 1860er Jahren lebhaft und setzt sich bis zum Ende seines Schaffens in den 1890er Jahren fort. Farben, Linien und Stil seiner Arbeiten unterstrichen seine direkte Verbindung zur Natur; das machte seine Arbeiten im 19. Jahrhundert für viele so anziehend. Als die Städte immer mehr Raum einnahmen und die natürliche Umgebung weiter zurückwich, waren Morris' lebendige und ansprechende Muster für zahlreiche Menschen die einzige wirkliche Verbindung zur Natur. So ist es nicht verwunderlich, dass in der Viktorianischen Zeit viele ihr Zuhause mit den dekorativen Mustern von Morris schmückten, denn irgendwie brachten sie die Farben, die Bewegungen und Leuchtkraft der Natur ins Haus.
Deshalb sind auch so viele der dekorativen Arbeiten von Morris bis heute überliefert und so populär wie eh und je. Wir können sehen, welche Liebe Morris für die Natur empfand und welche tiefe Verbindung er zu ihr hatte. Seine Bewunderung für die Natur überdauert und lässt uns mit ihm in diese Bewunderung einstimmen.

Español

William Morris

William Morris (1834–1896) dijo en su célebre frase "No tengas nada en tu casa que no sea útil o no lo creas hermoso", y el hecho de que esta premisa orientara su trayectoria profesional dice mucho tanto del hombre en sí como del legado de su producción creativa.
William Morris fue uno de los diseñadores decorativos ingleses más importantes e influyentes del siglo XIX. Su obra como diseñador fue ingente, siendo el creador de centenares de diseños para telas tejidas y estampadas, bordados, tapices, papel pintado, vidrieras y ornamentación de libros, entre otros. La fama de sus patrones ha superado la prueba del paso del tiempo, manteniéndose durante generaciones como uno de los favoritos entre el gran público, los decoradores de interiores y los artesanos.
Tal y como se refleja en su obra, Morris sentía un profundo vínculo con el entorno natural. En muchos aspectos, sus patrones decorativos son una loa a la infinita diversidad de la campiña inglesa. Aunque en modo alguno puede decirse que sea el único diseñador cuyo patrón creativo personal haya sido la naturaleza, Morris se cuenta entre los mejores. Su comprensión íntima de la belleza presente en la naturaleza y de la manera en que dicha belleza puede conceptualizarse para luego ser estilizada con sencillez dentro de un patrón decorativo, hizo de Morris uno de los diseñadores victorianos de mayor renombre.
Es su evidente conocimiento íntimo, reconocimiento y admiración por el mundo natural lo que de forma tan vívida impregna toda la obra decorativa de Morris, desde sus primeros diseños en la década de 1860 hasta su muerte en 1896. Los colores, las líneas y los estilos de su obra ponen de relieve una conexión directa con la naturaleza, y son justamente estas cualidades las que llevaron a tantas personas a admirar su trabajo en el siglo XIX. A medida que la expansión de las ciudades provocaba el repliegue de la naturaleza, los vibrantes y atractivos patrones de Morris se convirtieron para muchos en su único punto de contacto con la naturaleza. En este sentido, no es extraño que en la época victoriana fueran tantos quienes tapizaran sus hogares con los patrones decorativos de Morris, pues de algún modo transmitían el color, el movimiento y la vitalidad de la naturaleza dentro del hogar.
Este es el motivo que explica la preservación de gran parte de la obra decorativa de Morris y el hecho de que siga siendo ahora tan popular como siempre. Morris nos hace testigos del amor que sintió por la naturaleza y de su comunión con ella. La admiración de este diseñador por el medio natural sigue ahí y su vigencia nos permite compartirla con él.

PEPIN®

Pepin® is a trademark of Pepin Holding BV

Published by
The Pepin Press BV
P.O. Box 10349
1001 EH Amsterdam, The Netherlands
mail@pepinpress.com

www.pepinpress.com

Art Direction / Cover Design
Pepin van Roojen

Introduction
John Hopper

ISBN 978 94 6009 079 0

This book is produced by The Pepin Press in Amsterdam and Singapore.